First Science Experiments

MIGHTY MACHINES

by **Shar Levine and Leslie Johnstone**

illustrations by **Steve Harpster**

Sterling Publishing Co., Inc.
New York

To Uncle Syd and Aunt Molly.—SL

To my dad, amongst other things, a great accountant, bike mechanic, carpenter, ski instructor, snooker player, bread and sushi maker, father, and grandfather. Thanks for teaching me too many things to mention in one book.—LJ

The authors wish to thank Frances X. Gilbert for her support.

Edited by Nancy E. Sherman

Library of Congress Cataloging-in-Publication Data
Levine, Shar. 1953-
   First science experiments : mighty machines / Shar Levine and Leslie Johnstone ; illustrated by Steve Harpster.
      p. cm.
   ISBN 1-4027-0900-5
   1. Simple machines Juvenile literature. I. Johnstone, Leslie. II. Harpster, Steve. III. Title.
TJ147 .L48 2004
621.8-dc22
                              2003025202

10 9 8 7 6 5 4 3 2

Published by Sterling Publishing Co., Inc.
387 Park Avenue South, New York, NY 10016
© 2004 by Shar Levine and Leslie Johnstone
Distributed in Canada by Sterling Publishing

c/o Canadian Manda Group,
One Atlantic Avenue, Suite 105
Toronto, Ontario, Canada M6K 3E7
Distributed in Great Britain and Europe
by Chris Lloyd at Orca Book Services,
Stanley House, Fleets Lane, Poole BH15 3AJ, England
Distributed in Australia by Capricorn Link (Australia) Pty. Ltd.
P.O. Box 704, Windsor, NSW 2756, Australia

Printed in China

Sterling ISBN 1-4027-0900-5

Contents

Note to Parents and Teachers

This book is designed to answer very basic questions young children have about simple machines. Children may never ask what a simple machine is, but they may want to know the difference between a screw and a nail or why a screw has ridges. All these answers lie in the realm of simple machines.

Simple machines are everywhere, but some may be cleverly disguised. A seesaw is just a lever and fulcrum. A wheelchair ramp is simply an inclined plane. And a crank is something more than a child who has not had enough sleep. This book may not answer all a child's questions about simple machines, but it's a good start. If your child wants to learn more about a specific topic, visit the library to find a book on the subject. Surf the Internet with your child; try using a search engine where you type in a question and get directed to sites that may provide answers. Make a list of your child's questions and work with her or him to find the answers. Think of all you may discover together!

Safety First: These activities are designed to be as safe and simple as possible. Some adult supervision is suggested with small children. Please read the **Be Safe** checklist with your child before starting any of the activities.

Be Safe

DO

✔ Before starting any activity, get an adult's okay to do it.

✔ Read through each activity with an adult first. It's best if the adult "helps" or stays nearby.

✔ Have an adult handle anything that is sharp or made of glass.

✔ Keep babies and pets away from experiments and supplies.

✔ Wash your hands when you are finished.

✔ Keep your work area clean. Wipe up spills right away.

✔ Tell an adult right away if you or anyone else gets hurt!

DON'T

✔ Don't put any part of these experiments in your mouth.

✔ Don't try to move or lift any objects before asking an adult if it is okay.

✔ Don't experiment with or take apart any object before you get an adult's permission.

✔ Never use a screwdriver on anything that plugs into the wall and never put anything made of metal into a wall outlet.

Introduction

Wouldn't it be great if you had a machine to do all your chores? A machine that would clear the table after meals, rake the lawn, take out the trash—even pick up your toys. Maybe you'd like this machine to tidy your room, wash your clothes, or sweep the floor. Wait! This machine would do lots of the things that your parents do every day. Too bad we don't yet have a chore machine, but we do have a lot of other machines that make life easier.

Close your eyes and think of a machine. What comes to mind? Do you think of a sewing machine? Perhaps a monster truck. You probably didn't think about the wedge holding open the door to your room. This book will teach you about simple machines—machines that pretty much live up to their name.

Before you look at the machines themselves, let's think a little bit about the way things move and what makes them move the way they do. For instance, have you ever wondered why basketballs don't

float up into the air like balloons? While you may think this is a silly thing to ask in a book about machines, there's a good reason for this seemingly illogical question. The answer lies in the science of **physics**. Physicists study how **forces** like **gravity** act on everything in the universe, including those basketballs. For one thing, it's gravity that keeps basketballs returning to Earth after a good bounce. So let's get started by discussing some of the basic ideas in physics (see bolded words in Glossary, page 47).

Force Fields

Say you are in a swimming pool and you push against the side of the pool. What happens? The pool doesn't move, but you do. Now if you push against a shopping cart, you'll see that it will move, but you will not. In both cases you exert a force, but different things happen...or do they?

You can describe a force as a push or a pull. Forces work on objects that are moving and objects that are standing still. They can cause objects to move or change direction. They can also make moving objects stop. You can feel a force acting on you when you hold something heavy or you are in a car that stops suddenly.

When a force acts on an object, the object puts out an equal force in the opposite direction. That's why when you pushed on the side of the pool, you moved. But the shopping cart had wheels and you had feet, so it moved instead of you.

This is the effect of **friction**. Friction slows an object's speed of motion—by just how much depends on the **weight** (or mass) of the object and the surfaces involved. More mass, more friction; the reverse is also true. Smoother surface, less friction. A wheel, being smooth and round, reduces friction; feet in shoes cause more friction. Between you and the shopping cart, it's no contest.

So, why more mass, more friction? Because of another force called gravity. An object that has mass attracts other objects; it pulls them toward itself. How hard it pulls depends on the size of the object doing the pulling. Earth is enormous, so it pulls very hard; it has a huge force of gravity. Even though you may see balloons floating up and away, once the helium escapes them, they fall back to Earth.

How can I weigh really small things?

For the projects in this book, you need a scale to weigh things, but a bathroom scale doesn't really work. It's better to use what's called a spring scale. The easiest spring scale to find is the kind used for fishing. It works like this: to weigh something, like a small toy, just attach the toy to the hook on the scale and lift it up. The spring stretches and the arrow or marker points to the correct weight. But what if no one at your house fishes? You can always make your own spring scale.

You need

* rubber band   * paper clip
* ruler with a hole in one end
* weight from page 14 (plastic bag and rice)

Do this

1 Poke the rubber band through the hole in the ruler and pull one end of the rubber band through the other. Tug gently to make a big loop.

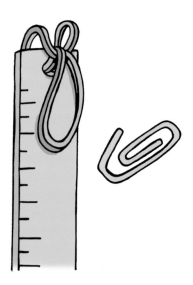

2 Straighten the paper clip, keeping the hook shapes at the ends. Put one hook through the looped rubber band.

3 Now weigh something: slip the other paper clip hook through a hole in the plastic bag filled with rice and let it hang down along the ruler. Note where the weight rests on the ruler.

4 Open the bag and remove some of the rice. Attach the weight to the paper clip again and see where it stops along the ruler.

What happened?

You made a spring scale. The rubber band hanging down along the ruler acts like a spring and the marks on the ruler give you a rough idea of how much the thing weighs.

Simple Machines

Before you can understand how simple machines work, you need to know what work is. No, you don't have to get a job; you just have to know how scientists use the word "work." Work means moving a thing by pushing or pulling it over a distance.

A simple machine is a thing that makes work easier. It may have few—or even no—moving parts. You may think that machines have engines and lots of metal parts. Yes, a lot of them do, but don't be fooled. Even your front teeth are a kind of simple machine.

There are six basic types of simple machine: ramps, **screws**, and **wedges**, all belonging to a group called inclined planes. **Levers**, **wheels** and **axles**, and **pulleys** are members of the lever family. Any of these simple machines can make work easier by helping you move objects using less muscle.

Levers

Like you, levers belong to families sharing similar features. The feature that all levers share is a bar that balances or turns on a fixed base or pivot called a **fulcrum**. There are three families or classes of lever and each one has the fulcrum in a different place.

It's easy to picture a first-class lever; just look at a seesaw. The fulcrum is in the middle. A heavier person (the load) always moves downward and a lighter one (the effort) up. Move the heavier person toward the middle and the lighter one can lift the heavier. The closer the load to the fulcrum, the less the effort needed.

For a second-class lever, picture a nutcracker. The fulcrum is at one end (where the rods meet); the effort (your hand) is at the other. The nut (the load) is in between. If you've ever used a nutcracker, you know that it works best when the nut is closest to the fulcrum (the joint).

A toilet handle that you push down at one end is a third-class lever. The attached end is the fulcrum, the middle of the handle is the load, and your hand on the end is the effort.

How do different levers work

Here's a simple way to see the three different classes of lever at work.

You need

★ rice　　★ rubber band　　★ chair

★ resealable plastic sandwich bag

★ fish or spring scale (see page 10)

★ measuring stick or wooden dowel

★ adult helper

Do this

1 Make a weight: fill the plastic sandwich bag with rice and seal it. Place a rubber band around the bag and hang the weight by the rubber band.

2 Hold the stick steady across the back of the chair. Ask an adult to attach the weight to one end of the stick. Attach the fish scale to the other end of the stick. Pull down on the scale to lift the bag

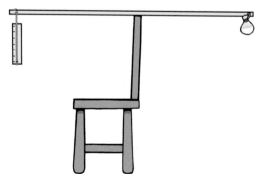

of rice at the other end. Have an adult help you read the scale. This is a first-class lever.

3 Move the stick so that only the end of it hangs over the chair back. Have an adult attach the weight to the middle of the stick. Use the fish scale to hold the stick level. What does the scale show now? This is a second-class lever.

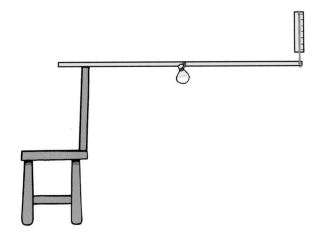

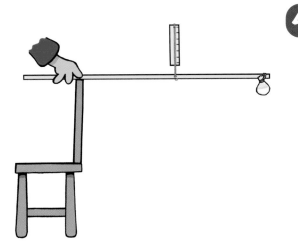

4 Have an adult move the weight to the end of the stick. Place the fish scale in the middle. Have a helper hold the end of the stick on the chair so it doesn't come up. Lift the scale until the stick is horizontal. This is a third-class lever.

Can I use parts of my body as levers?

Do you like to play sports? Can you hit a softball out into left field or a slapshot in hockey? What do these games have to do with levers, anyway? Let's find out.

You need

* large, flat surface like a playground or backyard
* hockey stick or baseball bat
* measuring tape
* tennis ball or other small ball
* masking tape

Do this

1 Find a large, flat space, like an empty field. Use masking tape to make a big X on the ground. Place the ball on the X.

2 Put one hand at the top of the hockey stick, about 1 inch (2.5 cm) from the end. Place your other hand around the stick as far down as you can reach. Take aim at the ball and hit it. Measure how far the ball went.

3 Find the ball and place it back on the X. Move your bottom hand up a little on the stick or bat and hit the ball again. Did it go farther this time?

4 Keep hitting the ball as you move your hand up or down the hockey stick or baseball bat. How is it easiest to hit the ball? With your hands in which position did the ball travel farthest?

What happened?

Where you placed your hands changed the distance that the ball traveled. The hockey stick or baseball bat acts as a third-class lever. The ball is the load force at one end of the stick, your bottom hand provides the effort force in the middle, and the fulcrum is at the top, where your other hand stays still. When your bottom hand is closer to the ball, you can't hit the ball as hard—the distance between the effort and the load is too short. You have no *leverage*. As you move your hand up the stick or the bat, the distance grows and you can hit the ball farther.

Pulleys

What is the easiest way to lift something heavy? Just ask your older sister or brother for help, of course. That was painless. But what if that isn't an option? You can always use a pulley.

A pulley is a simple machine made by looping a cord or belt around a support. The support is usually one or more grooved wheels that turn smoothly and allow the belt or cord to move easily through or around them. Some pulleys move and are called movable pulleys. Others stay in one place; these are fixed pulleys. Often several pulleys are linked together to do more complex tasks.

Over 2,000 years ago, a Greek scientist by the name of Archimedes was the first person to study the way levers work. He dared to boast that with a lever big enough, he could lift the world. What he meant was that if he had a long enough lever and someplace out in space to put the fulcrum, he could move the Earth. Archimedes is also famed for jumping out of the bathtub and running naked down the street yelling "Eureka!" ("I have found it!" in Greek) when he figured out the answer to another scientific puzzle. He was one smart but really strange dude.

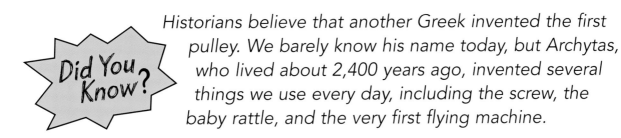

Historians believe that another Greek invented the first pulley. We barely know his name today, but Archytas, who lived about 2,400 years ago, invented several things we use every day, including the screw, the baby rattle, and the very first flying machine.

How can I lift up something really heavy?

How do people move pianos and heavy furniture into tall buildings? It's easy if the thing fits inside the elevator or they can carry it up the stairs. If not, they might use a simple machine.

You need

* empty thread spool
* 2 chairs the same height
* ribbon just thinner than the spool
* 2 plastic pails with handles
* string
* broom
* pennies or marbles

Do this

1 Run a piece of string about 1 foot (30 cm) long through the hole in the spool and tie the ends of the string together.

2 Slide the spool and string onto the broom handle. Rest the handle across the two chairs with the spool hanging between.

3 Put one pail on the floor and tie the end of a piece of ribbon to its handle.

4 Slide the other end of the ribbon over the spool and tie it to the handle of the other pail, which should dangle in the air.

5 Add a few pennies to the hanging pail. What happens to the pail on the ground?

6 Return the pail to the ground and add a handful of pennies or marbles. Pull the handle of the hanging pail toward the ground. What happens to the pail filled with weights?

What happened?

As you added pennies to the hanging pail, it started to lift up the pail on the ground. A single fixed pulley lets you pull in one direction to move a thing in the other direction. This is handy: it means you don't have to climb up a flagpole to raise the flag. Instead, you can stand safely on the ground and pull on the rope as the flag rises to the top.

Can I lift a weight with a pulley that moves?

In the last activity, you lifted a weight with a pulley that hung in place in the air. But how would it work if your pulley could move?

You need

- ✲ plastic pail with handle
- ✲ empty thread spool
- ✲ ribbon just thinner than the spool
- ✲ pennies or marbles
- ✲ string
- ✲ tape

Do this

1. Place some marbles or pennies in the pail. Lift the pail into the air and note how heavy it is.

2. Run a piece of string about 1 foot (30 cm) long through the hole in the spool, then through the pail handle. Tie the ends together.

3. Tape one end of the ribbon to the top of a table or counter near the edge. Since tape can leave a mark, ask an adult before you do this. If you can't use tape, have an adult or a friend hold the end of the ribbon on the table.

4. Run the ribbon underneath and through the groove in the spool.

5 Pull up gently on the ribbon until it lifts the pail. Does it seem lighter than when you just lifted the pail by itself?

What happened?

You made a movable pulley. In the last activity, the pulley was fixed: it stayed in place up near the broom handle. In this activity, the pulley moved as you pulled up on the ribbon. When you lifted the pail by itself, you didn't have to move your hand very far, but the pail was heavier. When you used the pulley, you needed to move your hand a little farther, but the pail seemed to weigh only half as much. With a movable pulley, the weight is distributed over, or supported by, all the belts (or ribbons). Your pulley had two supporting belts, one from the table to the pulley, and one from the pulley to your hand. This made the pail seem to weigh only half as much. And moving it seemed to be only half the work!

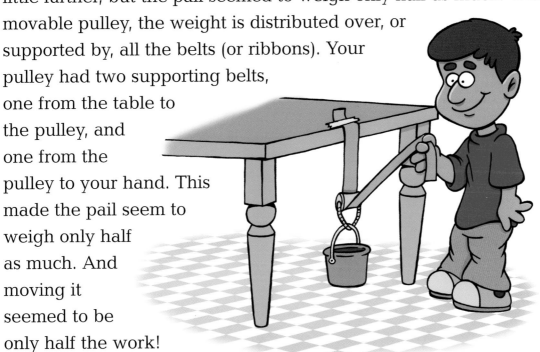

Wheels and Axles

It isn't known who invented the wheel, but the wheel by itself isn't much use. You have to attach something to it. Take a round candy with a hole in the middle and try to move something with it. You don't get very far, do you? Now place a thin pretzel in the hole as an axle and roll the candy around. This time you get somewhere. So a better question might be who invented the wheel and axle?

The wheel and axle is made from a large diameter disk (the wheel) and a smaller diameter shaft or rod (the axle). The outside edge of the wheel travels a much longer distance than the outside of the axle.

While you may know a "crank" as someone who is in a bad mood, there's another meaning for the word. A crank is a handle used to turn an axle. A peppermill uses an example of a crank. When you turn the handle, it turns the mill (axle) to grind the pepper.

Did you ever wonder how the treadmill, a modern kind of exercise machine, got its name? Turns out a treadmill was used to mill, or grind, grains. Several men would walk inside something resembling a "hamster wheel." As they walked, they turned the wheel, which was attached to an axle that went to a gear (a wheel with teeth) that turned the stone that ground the grain to make flour.

A yo-yo also acts like a wheel and axle, only with the yo-yo, the wheel is being turned by the axle. The string of the yo-yo isn't tied to the wheel directly; it's attached to the axle with a loop. When you pull on the string, it turns the axle in the middle of the toy that makes the wheel turn a greater distance.

Then the wheel spins and makes the axle turn and the whole thing rises up the string into the air.

Why do you need both a wheel and an axle?

A wheel is great for spinning around, but you'd have a hard time moving anything with a wheel alone. To move things with a wheel, you also need an axle.

You need
- 2 chairs with ladder backs
- broom handle
- string
- pail with handle
- masking tape
- safety scissors
- ruler

Do this

1 Place the chairs back to back, about 1 foot (30 cm) apart. Rest the broom handle across two level slats.

2 Tie a 1 foot (30 cm) length of string to the pail handle. Tape the free end of the string to the middle of the broom handle.

3 Place some pennies or marbles in the pail to make it heavier.

4 Turn the broom handle with your hands to raise the pail into the air. Turn it back the other way to return the pail to the ground.

5 Tape the ruler straight up and down on the broom handle near one end, as shown above.

6 Use the ruler, which acts as a wheel, to turn the broom handle and lift the pail.

What happened?

You lifted the pail either way, but it saved you effort in lifting the pail when you used the ruler (the wheel) to turn the broom handle (the axle). Your hand had to move further when you used the ruler, but the force you needed was less—the pail seemed lighter. The ruler acted as a bigger wheel, and the bigger the wheel, the easier it is to lift the load. And that is the purpose of a labor-saving device.

Why can't I put in a screw with my fingers ?

One familiar tool you probably have somewhere at home is a screwdriver. This is another simple machine; it's based on the wheel and axle. Here's how it works.

You need

★ screw   ★ screwdriver to fit the screw
★ piece of Styrofoam™ about 1 inch (2.5 cm) thick

Do this

1 Gently push the pointed end of the screw just a little way into the Styrofoam.

2 Try to turn the screw using only your fingers. Don't hammer it in with a heavy object. Does the screw go into the Styrofoam?

3 Now try to turn the screw with the screwdriver. Does it go into the Styrofoam now?

What happened?

You discovered why it's called a screwdriver. You found it was hard, maybe even impossible, to twist the screw in with just your fingers. But the screwdriver easily drove the screw into the Styrofoam. That's because the screwdriver and the screw act like a wheel and axle. The screwdriver (the wheel) is bigger around than the screw (the axle). You have to twist the handle of the screwdriver a greater distance to turn the screw a fairly short distance, but it doesn't take as much effort. Remember, the whole idea is to make the work easier.

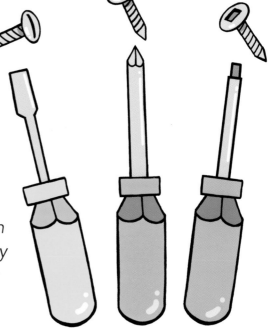

Did You Know?

There are many kinds of screwdrivers. A flat-head screwdriver has a flat top edge, a Phillips screwdriver has an X shape, and a Robertson has a square top. All these screwdrivers come in different sizes too, just like the screws they fasten. What kinds of screwdrivers do you have at home?

Inclined Planes

Inclined planes or ramps are something you see every day. They're often at the corners of city sidewalks, where they let wheelchairs move more easily off and on. Skateboarders do some awesome tricks off larger curved wooden ramps. And if you like to snowboard, you may someday try the huge half pipes, which are frozen ramps. Watch the winter Olympics or a TV show covering this sport and you'll see people fly!

Basically, a ramp or inclined plane is a sloping surface along which a load can be moved. The more gentle the slope, the more easily the load is moved, but the longer the distance.

An interesting thing about these simple machines is that, unlike pulleys, screws, and levers, inclined planes have no moving parts.

Did You Know? The ancient Greeks told of a trickster king named Sisyphus (sis'-i-fus). Sisyphus tricked death, which angered the gods. As punishment, he was condemned forever to push a heavy rock up a hill (an inclined plane, by the way). As soon as the rock reached the top of the hill, it would roll right back down to the bottom again, and poor Sisyphus would have to start all over. Too bad he didn't know how to build a simple machine.

How did they build tall buildings? before they had cranes

All over the world, ancient peoples built huge structures. There are the great pyramids of Egypt and equally impressive ones built by the Mayans in Mexico. But how did builders in these early cultures move the materials to the building site and lift them into place without modern construction equipment?

You need

* several large books
* spring scale   * small toy car or truck
* board about 18 inches (45 cm) long
* rice/plastic bag weight from page 14

Do this

1 Stack the books on the table near the table's edge. Lean the board on the table against the books to create a ramp.

2 Place the weight on the table against the bottom of the ramp. Use the spring scale to drag the weight up the ramp. Have an adult help you read the scale.

3 Place the weight on the table and lift it to the same height as in Step 2, using the spring scale. What does the scale read now?

4 Balance the weight atop a small toy car or truck. Use the spring scale to drag the weighted toy up the ramp. Was it easier to drag the weight on wheels?

5 Add or take away books to raise or lower the ramp. Does this change the effort you have to make to lift the weight?

What happened?

It was the same amount of work, but it was easier to drag the weight up the ramp than to lift it straight up. On wheels, the work is even easier, because the wheels reduce friction. The lower the stack of books (the more flat the ramp), the less force is needed to move the weight. A higher stack of books (a steeply sloping ramp) means you must use greater force to move the object.

Why are some ramps really long and others really short ?

If you've ever gone to an event in a large sports stadium, you may have walked up several levels of long, sloping ramps. Why do you think these ramps are designed this way?

You need

* board 4 feet (1.2 m) long
* several thick books
* rice/plastic bag weight (page 14)
* board 2 feet (60 cm) long
* fish or spring scale
* ruler

Do this

1 Stack the books so they reach a height of about 1 foot (30 cm).

2 Lean the short piece of wood against the stack of books to create a steep ramp.

3 Attach the scale to the weight and drag the weight up the ramp from the bottom. Ask an adult to help you read the scale.

4 Replace the short piece of wood with the long piece of wood and try the activity again. Was it easier this time or harder to drag the weight up the ramp?

What happened?

The weight reached the same height both times, but it was easier to drag the weight up the longer ramp than the shorter. You had to move the weight farther with the long ramp but it was easier. The shorter ramp took less time and distance, but it took greater effort.

In sports stadiums, many people have to move up and down the ramps. It is easier and faster for them to walk on long, gently sloping ramps than to walk up and down stairs or short, steep ramps.

Wedges

While wedges and inclined planes may look somewhat alike, these simple machines are used very differently. An inclined plane always stays in one place as objects move along its sloping surface. A wedge on the other hand is an inclined plane that moves.

A wedge often has two sides that slope or curve, while an inclined plane has only one. A wedge is pushed into objects to split them or to keep them from moving. A doorstop is a wedge; it's used to keep a door from banging shut. Axes split logs and knives cut vegetables, and both are wedges. Even your front teeth act as wedges when you bite into a carrot.

Wedges work because they are thin at one end and thicker at the other. You can feel that your upper front teeth curve from top to bottom; they are thinner at the bottom edge, where they penetrate the food. They become thicker toward the top, where they meet your gums. It's their shape that makes you able to pierce an apple and take off bites of a chewable size.

Most of the things used for cutting have a wedge shape. Axes, knives, and scissors are all wedges. One common thing you probably wouldn't even guess was a wedge is the zipper. When you look at a zipper, you see a row of "teeth" on either side of the fabric. To close a zipper, you run a slider along the sides of the metal or plastic edges (the teeth). Two wedge-shaped pieces inside the slider push the teeth together to lock the zipper. To open the zipper, the wedge shapes inside the slider pull the teeth apart.

Did You Know?

How do wedges work?

Why do wedges have to be thin at one end and thicker at the other?
What difference does it make?

You need

* sharpened pencil
* new unsharpened pencil
* 1 inch (2.5 cm) thick piece of Styrofoam
* thick piece of corrugated cardboard

Do this

1 Try to push the end of the new unsharpened pencil into a piece of Styrofoam. Does it go in easily? Try this again with a piece of corrugated cardboard. Does the unsharpened pencil go into the cardboard?

2 Keeping your hands away from the surface, try to push the end of the sharpened pencil into the Styrofoam and then into the cardboard. Does the pencil go into the objects this time?

What happened?

When you used the pencil with the flat end, it was nearly impossible to pierce the cardboard or the Styrofoam. But the sharpened pencil could easily be driven into the objects. In fact, the harder you pushed the end of the pencil, the further it penetrated. The sharp end of the pencil is a wedge, just like the ones used to split logs. The wedge changes the direction of the force: you push down but the wedge pushes down and *sideways*, against the material on either side. This allows the sharpened pencil to move in or penetrate. The longer and narrower the wedge, the easier it is to push into something.

Screws

A screw looks kind of like a nail with rough edges. Instead of a smooth surface, a screw has a series of ridges along its sides. Though it may be hard to believe, this is another simple machine, and one you probably use every day.

Just grab a bottle of soda and undo the cap. Look at the inside of the cap and the outside of the bottle's mouth. See those lines? That's a kind of screw. Do you have a spiral slide at your playground? That's a kind of screw, too.

Screws are really useful for holding things in place. Push a cork into the mouth of a bottle, then try to pull it out. It's not that hard, is it? Now try to pull off the cap from a closed bottle of pop. You can't. The screw's ridges hold the cap tightly in place. So just what are screws and how do they work?

Try to imagine a screw as an inclined plane that winds around a shaft or rod with a wedge at the tip. The wedge is the pointed end. The inclined plane is the ridge (or thread) that wraps around the screw. So a screw is like a ramp that wraps around a nail.

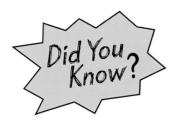

These devices all use screws.

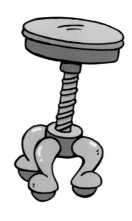

Remember Archimedes, the Greek scientist who liked to run naked through the streets (see page 19)? Well, not only did he explain how levers work, he also invented the Archimedes screw. This screw wasn't the metal kind you've been working with; it was designed to lift water from lakes or wells. In case you were wondering, Archimedes didn't name the screw after himself; someone else named it that in honor of him.

How do the ridges on screws work?

You've seen earlier (on page 28) that you can't really put in a screw with just your fingers. You need a screwdriver (acting as a wheel or crank) to do the job. But it wasn't just the greater force applied by the screwdriver that drove in the screw. The ridges helped.

If you look closely at a screw, you'll see a raised spiral winding around its body. Trace this spiral from the pointed end of the screw to the top and you'll find that it's one long line, not a series of circles. What's the point of these ridges anyway?

You need
* screws of several different sizes
* screwdriver
* 1 inch (2.5 cm) thick piece of Styrofoam

Do this

1 Push the point of a screw into the Styrofoam and turn it in using the screwdriver. Note how easily it goes in.

2 Choose another screw with many more ridges and one about

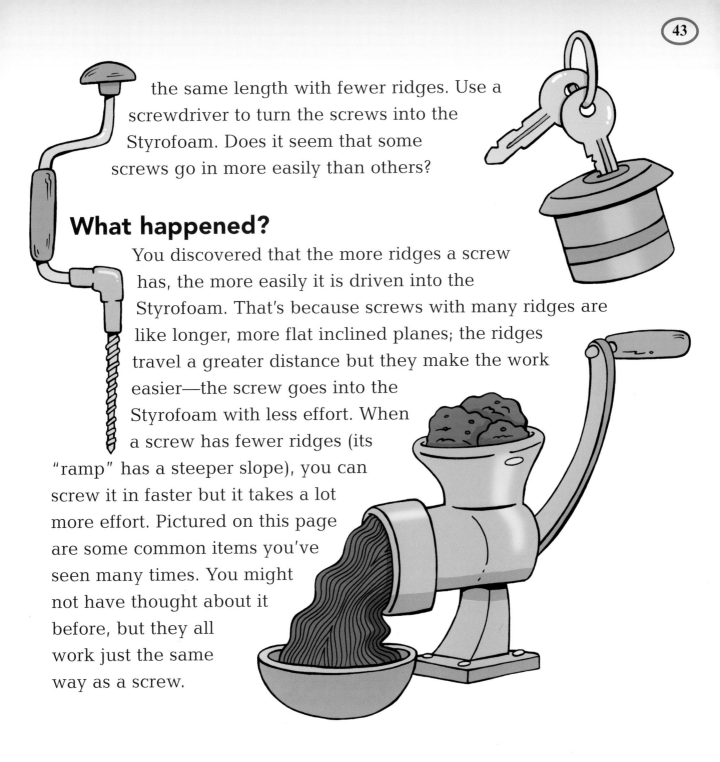

the same length with fewer ridges. Use a screwdriver to turn the screws into the Styrofoam. Does it seem that some screws go in more easily than others?

What happened?

You discovered that the more ridges a screw has, the more easily it is driven into the Styrofoam. That's because screws with many ridges are like longer, more flat inclined planes; the ridges travel a greater distance but they make the work easier—the screw goes into the Styrofoam with less effort. When a screw has fewer ridges (its "ramp" has a steeper slope), you can screw it in faster but it takes a lot more effort. Pictured on this page are some common items you've seen many times. You might not have thought about it before, but they all work just the same way as a screw.

What would you get if you unraveled a screw?

Would you ever think that a staircase is anything like a screw? You might if you've ever seen a spiral staircase. You could climb one of these to get to the top of a tall building (it's like a screw with the ridges inside)...or you could walk miles up a gently sloping ramp.

You need

- unsharpened pencil with an eraser at the end
- 2 foot (60 cm) long piece of string
- thumbtack
- ruler
- helper

Do this

1 Push the thumbtack into the end of the eraser on the pencil.

2 Tie one end of the string around the thumbtack.

3 Hold the pencil upright on its unsharpened end and draw out the string so that the loose end reaches the table. Have a helper use a ruler to measure the distance from the pencil to the end of the string. Look at the string and pencil from the side. What shape does it form?

4 Hold the loose end of the string in one hand and rotate or spin the pencil. The string should begin to wind around the pencil in a spiral.

What happened?

The pencil with the string stretched out looked just like an inclined plane. And when you wound the string around the pencil, you had a screw! A screw is basically an inclined plane wrapped around a rod. Screws can go into very hard materials like wood or metal and they hold very securely. Just think about how small a screw is. If buildings had long ramps instead of staircases, the ramps might go on for miles.

Compound Machines

What happens when you put two or more simple machines together? You get a compound machine. Some examples of compound machines (pictured here and on page 47) are a can opener and a construction crane.

The champion of compound machines was an artist named Rube Goldberg. He even inspired a Rube Goldberg contest where people try to come up with the strangest machine or most unlikely way to do a simple task.

Glossary

axle–a rod connected to a wheel or on which a
wheel turns

force–a push or pull that moves or alters
the course of an object

friction–a force that slows the relative
motion of objects against each other

fulcrum–the support on which a lever turns or moves

gravity–a force that pulls objects toward a body with great mass

gear–a wheel with teeth that turns something else

lever–a bar moving about a fixed point called a fulcrum that allows
an object at one point on the bar to be lifted by an effort exerted at
a different point on the bar

physics–the science dealing with the properties, changes, and
interactions of objects and energy

pulley–a wheel with a groove that allows a belt to move a load

screw–machine with a grooved thread that fastens objects together

wedge–tapered object used to cut or split, or to hold a thing in place

weight–the force of gravity working on an object, as measured on a
scale

wheel–a circular disk connected to an axle

Index